GLASS
AND
GRAVEL

Copyrights

Illustrations by Clara Vecchi
https://claravecchi.my.canva.site/ or scan:

Editing by Tereza Krasteva
Co-editing by Casey Leming
Formatting by Nick Calder
Sponsoring by Big Mouthwash

Published by Rerolling Human LLC
Use of this work in any way that enables or results in the training or development of artificial intelligence models is expressly prohibited without the publisher's prior written consent.

Visit the Author website at: NickCalderAuthor.com
Visit the Publisher at rerollinghuman.com (Under Construction)
Find more about the book at: glassandgravelbook.com

All names, characters, and incidents portrayed in this production are potentially fictitious. No identification with actual persons (living, deceased, or however they choose to identify), places, mythical beings, buildings, and products is intended or should be inferred unless it is or should be, or if truth is pragmatic.

First edition 2025

Paperback ISBN: 979-8-9917840-7-8
E-Book ISBN: 979-8-9917840-6-1

GLASS AND GRAVEL

Nick Calder

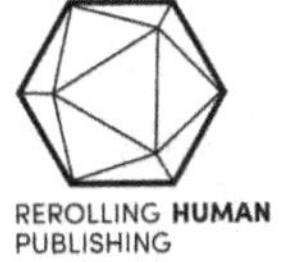

REROLLING **HUMAN**
PUBLISHING

DEDICATION

Thank you to all you before me who put your truth into the world, despite the risks, in the hope that it would help someone else. This book is only possible because of your sacrifices, and is one of my attempts at paying it forward.

Thank you to all you who supported me despite my flaws, and when I had nothing to offer you.

Thank you to all you who helped in the creation of this book, directly or indirectly.

Thank you to all you who believed me, or believed in me, when no one else did.

I couldn't have done this without you.
You know who you are.

Thank you to all you who chose to smear my name, despite your own guilt, in the hopes that you would benefit at my expense. The pain in this book is because of your lies. The successes in it are because I refused to pay it forward.

Thank you to all you who didn't believe me, or believe in me, because no one else did.

Thank you to all you who blamed me despite my innocence, when all I did was offer you everything I had.

Thank you to all you who earned my trust, only to use it against me.

I could have done this without you.
I just happened to do it despite you.
I know who you are.

TABLE OF CONTENTS

FOREWORD

Tereza Krasteva

Editor of 'The Brussels Review'

Poetry is the most intimate expression of one's hidden self. Humans find it unusual to evoke the deepest enigmatic introspections of their mind while facing a person's judgemental glare. This is why poetry exists—it is a tool of subjective revelation and a servant to the tortured psyche.

Yet, even poetry finds its constraints. Traditional form and structure have held the inherent freedom that poetry conjures in the shackles of outdated principles in literary expression.

Until now.

I first read this book in its most raw form. Here is what happened.

A
Sharp
Lashing tongue.

An open wound with words festering like maggots.
A frazzled mind reaching out like branches of a rotten tree.
Exposed organs squeezing themselves into oblivious annihilation.

As an author, you have to open your mouth and scream.
As an editor, you dig into lyrical mutilation and uncover its latent anatomy.
As a reader, you breathe in the thick aroma of worn pages and let it suffocate you.

Glass and Gravel is a botanical garden of interwoven maelstroms. *Glass and Gravel* is a dark forest drenched in heavy fog as it rains secrets and desires down a dehydrated throat. *Glass and Gravel* is the Earth's vital opening: an apotheosis of flesh revealed, a ribcage blooming into raw tongue, a wretched heart vessel, begging for the privilege of propagation.

I hope you feel it too.

How to Read This Poetry Book

For anyone who may find it helpful.
(If that's not you, turn to the next page.)

If poetry feels unfamiliar or intimidating, don't worry. Poetry isn't a puzzle you're required to solve—it's something to experience.

Here's one straightforward way to approach these poems:

1. **First Pass**: Read slowly without overthinking. Simply notice your reactions—confusion, curiosity, enjoyment, discomfort—all of it counts. Highlight or underline lines that catch your attention, even if you're unsure why.

2. **Second Pass (Recommended)**: Read the poem again, quietly to yourself or aloud. Let the poem's punctuation and spacing affect your reading however comes naturally; the meaning will become more apparent the less you try to fit it into what you already expect.

   Listen to its rhythm and feel how the words land differently the second time around.

3. **Third Pass (Optional)**: Explore your highlighted sections more deeply if you want. Jot down quick notes or questions about what resonates or puzzles you.

Interactive Opportunity:

I'd love to see what stood out to you and how each reading changed your experience. Share your highlights, questions, or reflections using #Glassandgravel on Instagram, X, or TikTok. Connect with fellow readers, see how each poem resonates differently for each of us, and become part of the conversation!

OPEN

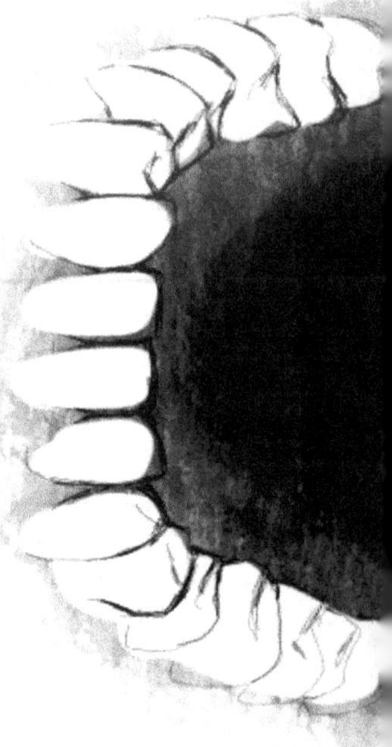

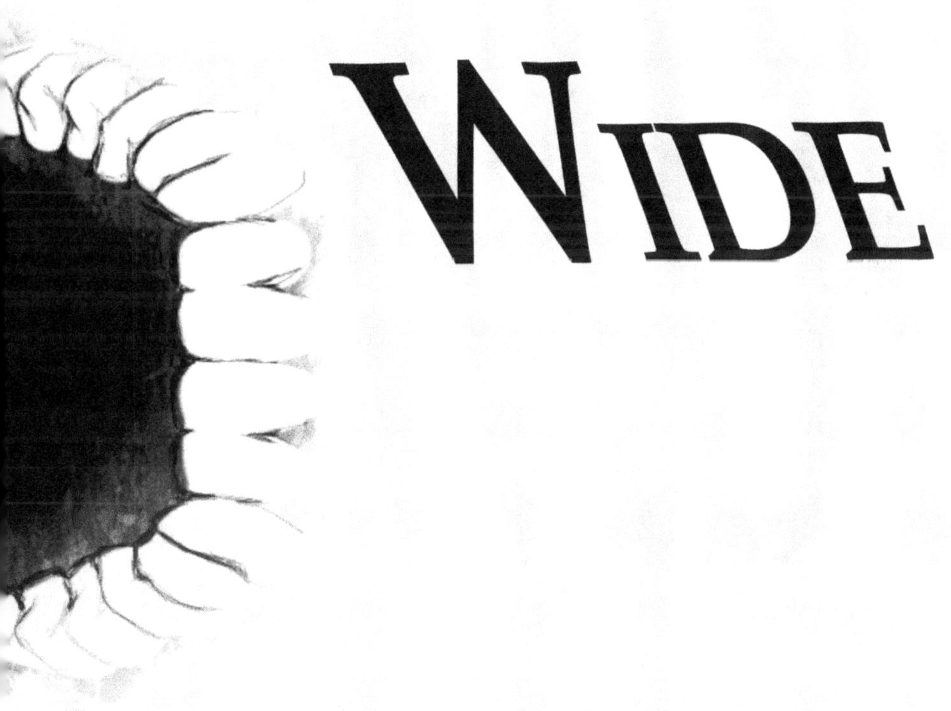

WIDE

WRITE A SHORT POEM. PROMPT: "HORIZON"

Part 1 of 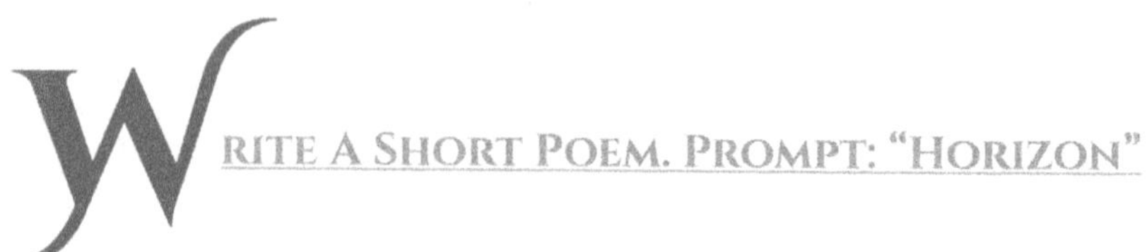

a jagged line devours the sea
stitching a seam in threads of fire.

I bystand barefoot on blistered earth
tasting the wind; *rust from distant storms*

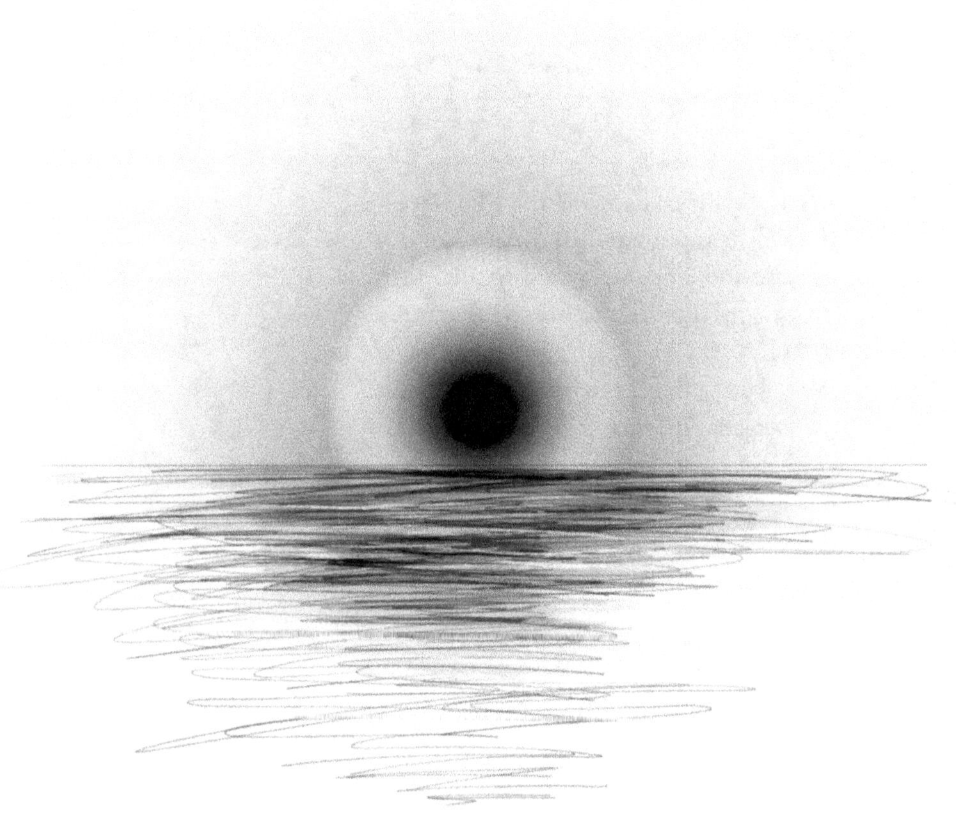

NICK CALDER

FAULT LINE

It's always there, something like sleep—
the World's split beneath the surface
the end and The End grinding their teeth
making mountains out of borrowed time.

We tell ourselves there isn't
a break; that it's just a shift
A Mother rearranges
her insides
to hold us   or all we bury

the stomach is a casket
for Sustenance;   quakes
un'neath the life. growth
and groans,   swallowing
hums of everything sworn

to keep but even

fertile ground can't bear
what begs to fracture thin
skin cracks and slither in
veins of truth too thick and thin

to pulse

blood wells in callous shells

Then,
it *ruptures* —

F

                              hells heave in and from raw iron lungs
whispers of walls echo cries in collapse
in slow motion, birth looks   Just   like death

        fates lie dark as secrets

orphans get tucked in beds;
 hunters love a Mistake
in crosshairs // (floaters are alive
                        in only your own eyes) // tent your palms

sweaty pray to catch

fallen skies with failed fists, *hear ye!*
                    hear ye, Earth's posthumous request;

        break.

now swallow— warm remembrance
                        immortalize the w hole, cold and in stone
your fossilized soul; compress it down to coal
        spark a midnight fire- let it steal the air, and leave

you

gasping for smoke

in the rubble of

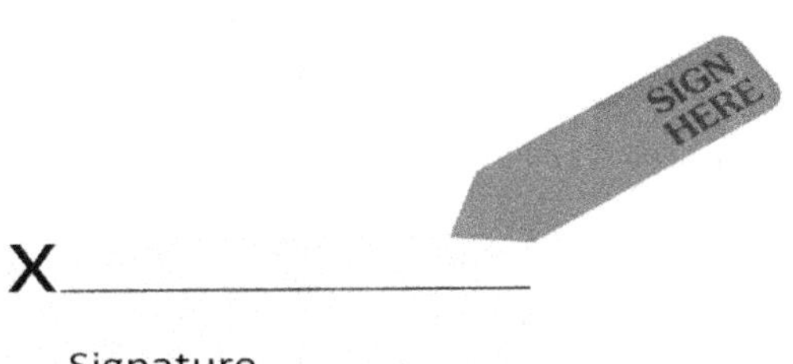

X________________________

Signature

F

—the rumbling ceased,   or eased
          I knelt,   or fell
   sifted debris,   or drowned

   felt the fault   inside Her womb
   throb *again* -   throb again—

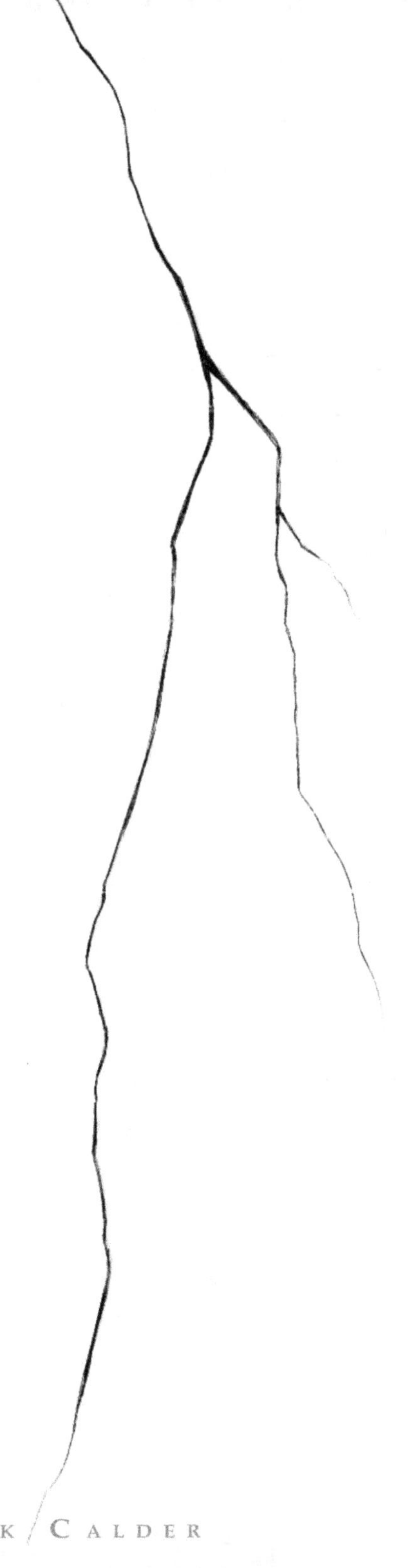

NICK / CALDER

Perennial Patterns

do you talk bad about me to your friends?

tremors in self
tangled in sheets
shitting the bed.

not opening
windows too oppressive
       too removed.

Still feeling Earth's posture
that it pardons magnetic pulls
of inexistence

(|Romulu?S|)

he? |Toil|(S
in) ?*his*? (cub)icle (C|Age|),
|Plot|ting the points,

he? |Toil|(S
in) ?*his*? (cub)icle (C|Age|),
|Plot|ting the points,

|(peer)|ing th[Rough] [Pane][Less]
(Gap)s
in [P(Ain]t)[Less] |Wall|s…

?he? [|Di-|]d [Not] for|get-| *gla*[|-*s*-|]*s*|,
?he?re[|-*member*|-]ed Abs[-en-]ce;

(-t)o imagine to *f*(*Eel*):

the |*breath*| *of* ?*sky*?|(*Scrap*)
e|*rs*[1] \ *bel*[*Low*]*s of* |*Moc*?¿*k*|-?|*ing*¿*birds*[2] /
the morning ?-[*night*]?*in*[*gale*][3] /.

[1]|Varicose| [as|Phalt|] (vein)s
[2]|Asthmatic| [(|Con|)crete] (lung)s
[3]|Mourning| [metal] *birds*

printing the (blue)
|plan|ning the [Off](Ice)
progres|sing| to the next…

re*membe*?ring? Absence,
|[Not] forgetting| (Mol-)(t(-e)n) (sand)s,

to |*Act*|*ual*ly |see|
?*life*?   (un-)|T(-i-)n(-t-)|(-ed)   by [Pane]s,
w?he?n the ?*found*?ation ?he? built

(Crumb)les.
|Crumble|s.

|Forget (Pain)t|

<u>STOP!</u>
THIS IS NOT A DRILL!
(OR A POEM)

The poem on the previous page has punctuation that, at first glance, may confuse you.

You can choose to read it in several ways.

- Come to your own conclusions on how to read it
  - (recommended for first read-through)
- Skip it
- Use the cheat sheet
  - (recommended after first read-through)

Why would I put a poem in the book if I was just going to tell you to skip it?

Where are you supposed to get this cheat sheet?

Access the cheat sheet, learn the hidden value behind including a poem people may skip, and gain some behind-the-scenes insights

Scan the QR code:

or follow the link: https://tally.so/r/wQErDg

Now, back to your regularly scheduled programming, with the talented Clara Vecchi, and your host:

Reflect

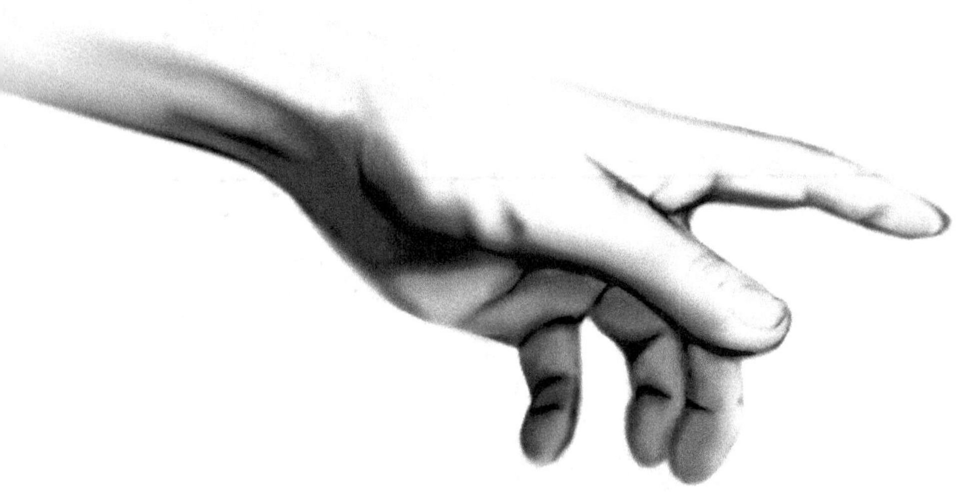

Reflect

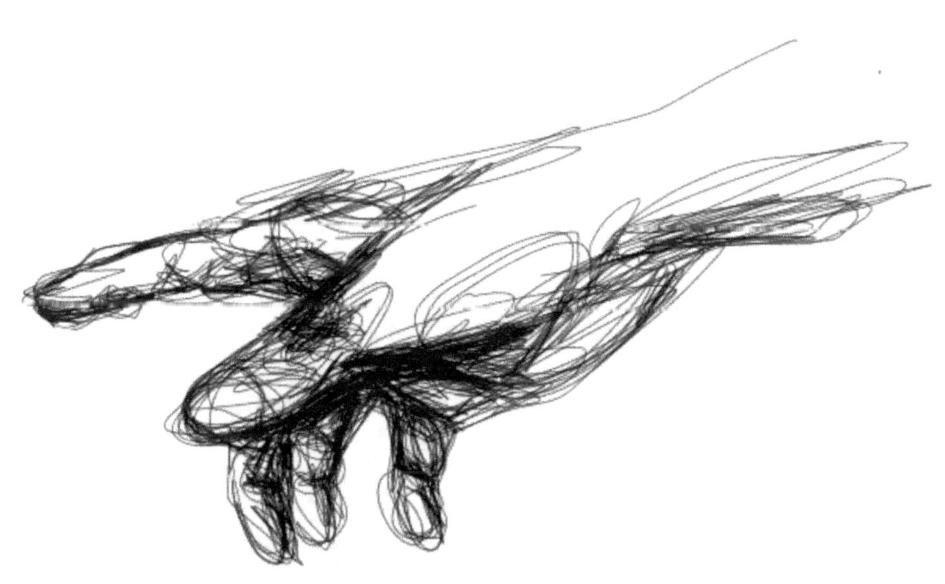

PAIN   †
staking intent
with grains
of sand; "turn glass"
he dreams.

She sways
like lavender. She paints
with bleach; "unsee"
She squeams.

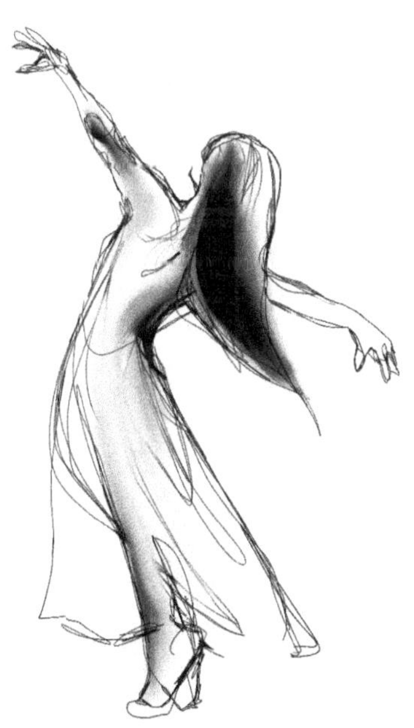

Pain

father Sun, flesh of Her
burns— fortune flogged, but *She* flays.
Lady Luck bandages his gashes
Gallant

improve
empower
emperfection
the scab for each abyss

PAIN

One upon once.
love   on   . time
the Sun. She paints
of Glass; then the beach

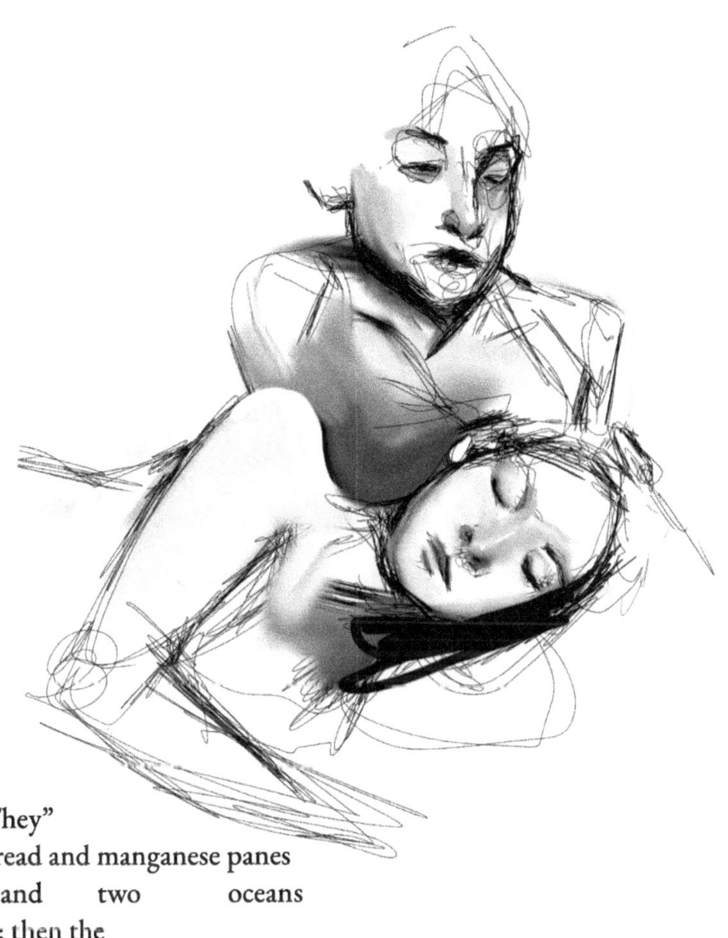

"draw They"
white bread and manganese panes
One   and   two   oceans
of Glass; then the
a moon?

Pain

the shatter water.

an altar
for each shard
even the*

Pain

AIN   †

    staking intent
      with grains
of sand; "turn glass"
he dreams.

She sways
like lavender. She paints
with bleach; "unsee"
She squeams.

father Sun, flesh of Her
burns— fortune flogged, but *She* flays.
Lady Luck bandages his gashes
Gallant

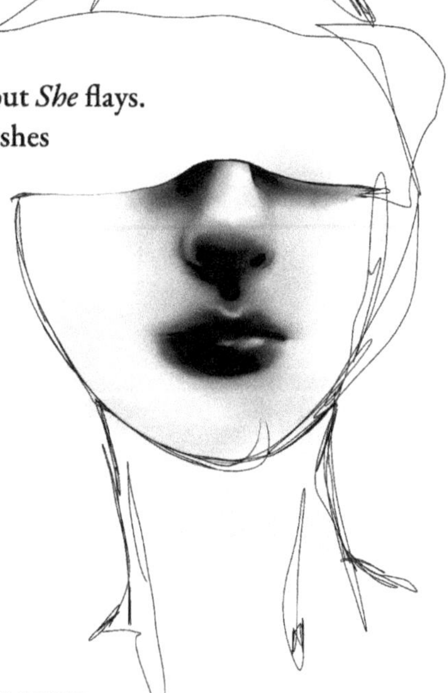

improve
empower
emperfection
the scab for each abyss

One upon once.
love   on   . time
the Sun. She paints
of Glass; then the beach

"draw They"
white bread and manganese panes
One   and   two   oceans
of Glass; then the
a moon?

the shatter water.

an altar
for each shard
even the*

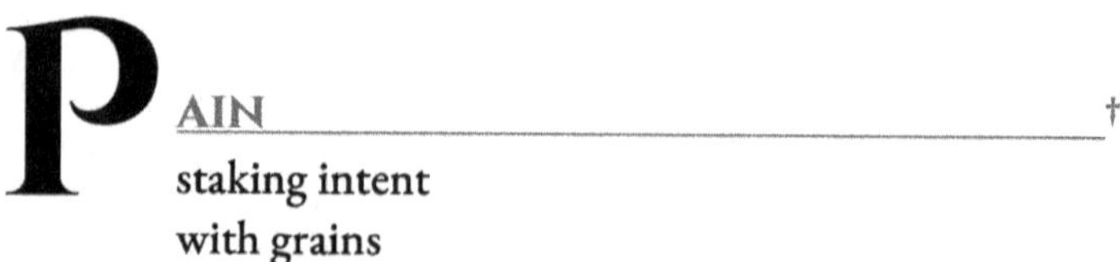

PAIN   †
staking intent
with grains

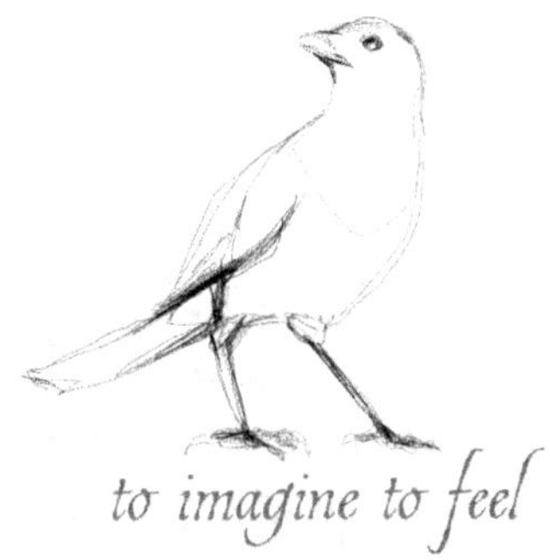

to imagine to feel

the breath of skyscrap
ers / bellows of mockingbirds /
the morning nightingale /

NICK CALDER

PIERCINGS

I built a home with walls of glass
to see the flowers but never touch
to never smell

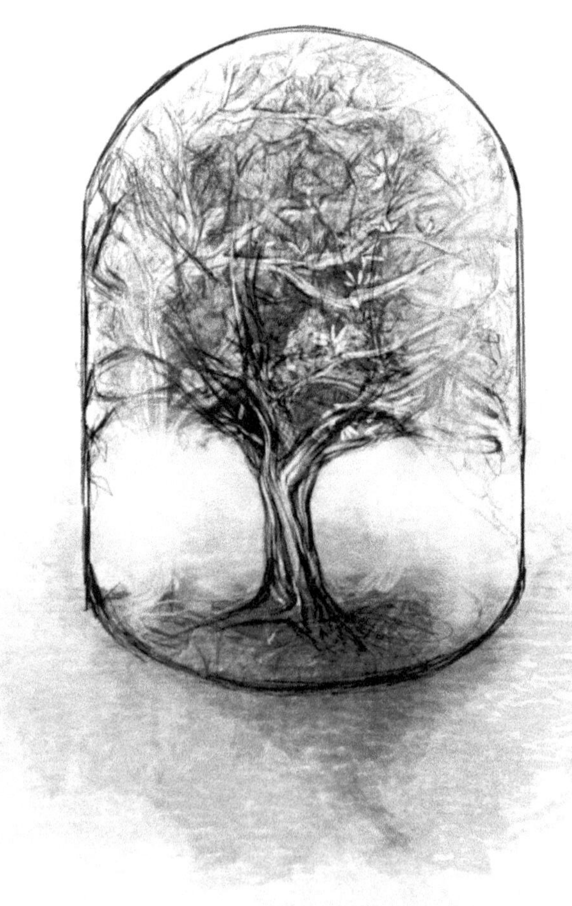

I built a house with stairs of glass
to see the grass but never touch
and never fell

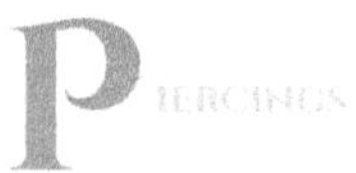

PIERCINGS

I built a love with stares of glass
I built a love with wails of glass
for the eyes' wells,
       they never wander

I hung portraits of almost-loves,
crooked faces on bent nails
broken frames and bloody nails

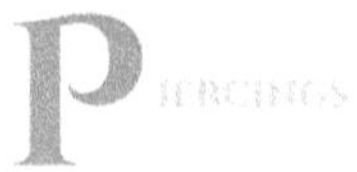

swept their shards into a mask;
pretend *I'm cleaning up my act!*
so The Nights can slip sockless

and pick my ghosts from Their soles

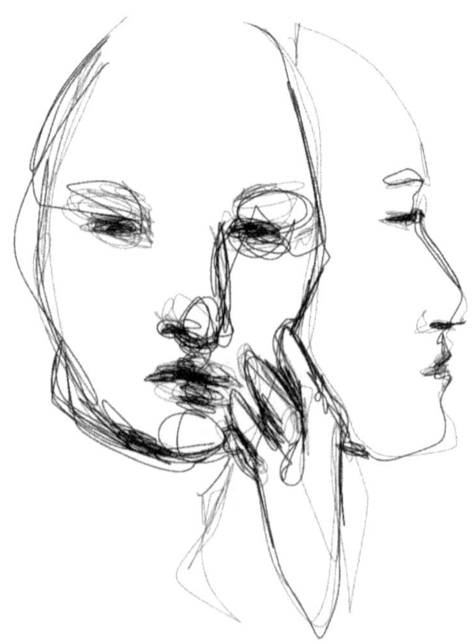

to lay in a bed of tempered lies
and search for an edge that might hold

                                            me

in fever-dreams; faces sweat like dew--

        cold,   close, and gone -

Piercings

by dawn. 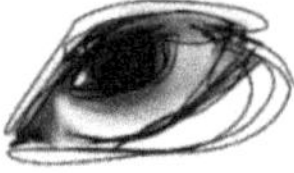

the portraits flinch. eyes crack
sand. mouths closed /split/ dry tongues—

spit

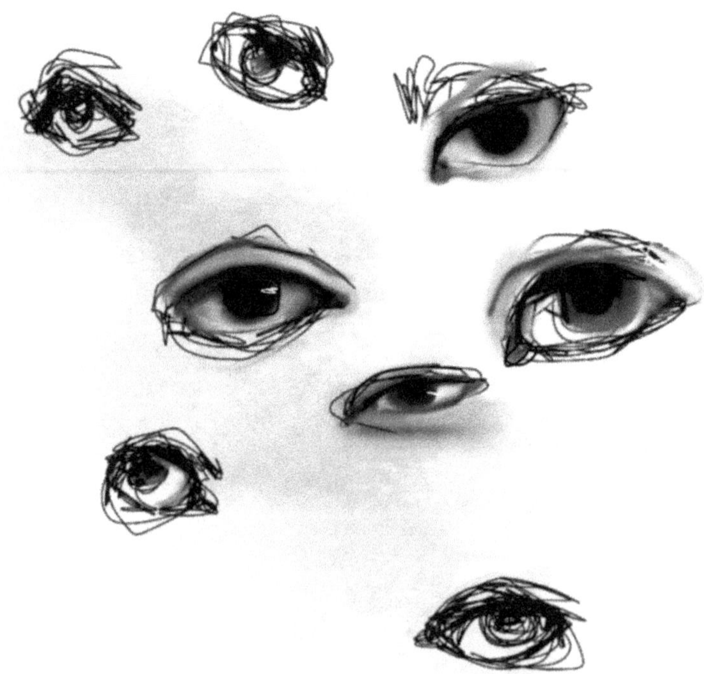

my name.   consecrating shame.
                  condensation;   my skin
                  crucifixion by whim   I hung

them anyway
        I hung

selves again. nails through glass—
reflections of skin
deep as beauty

in a yellow submarine

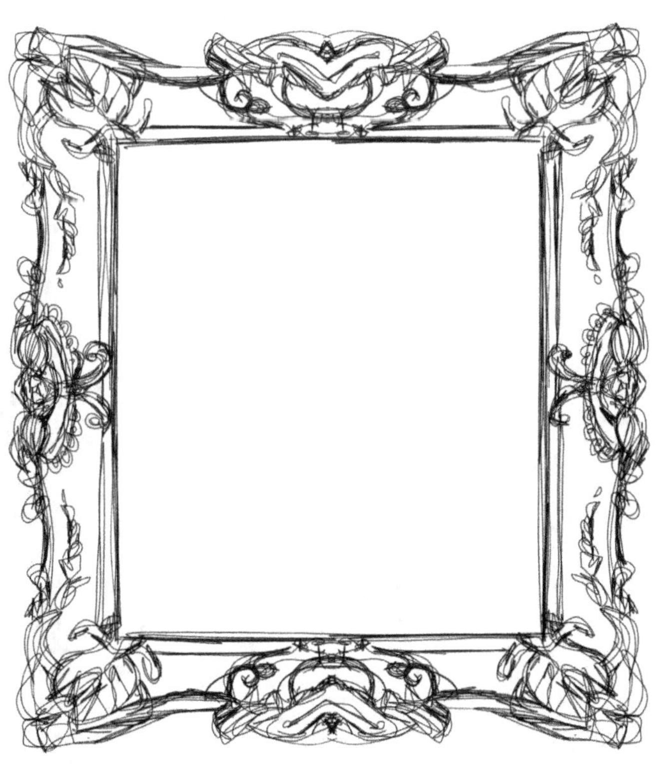

— "because empty nails

make *terrible* company"

– (*Romans 7:21-25*)

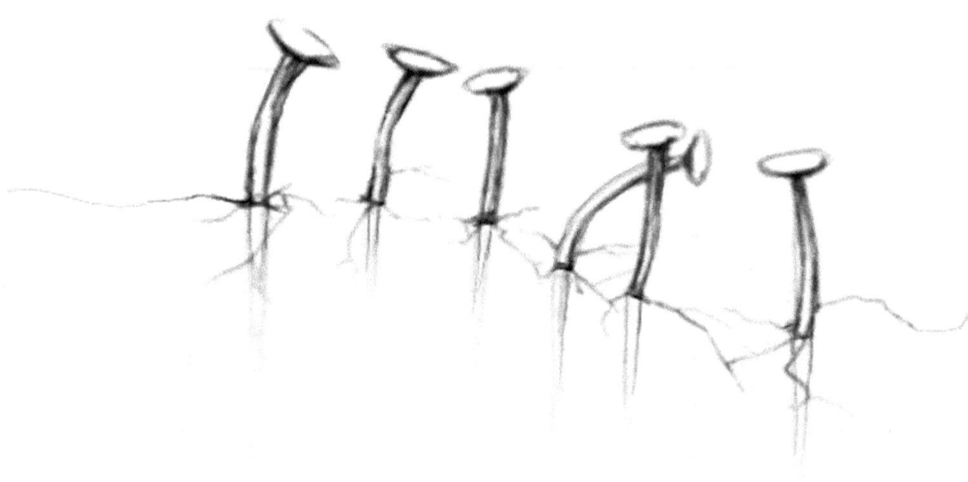

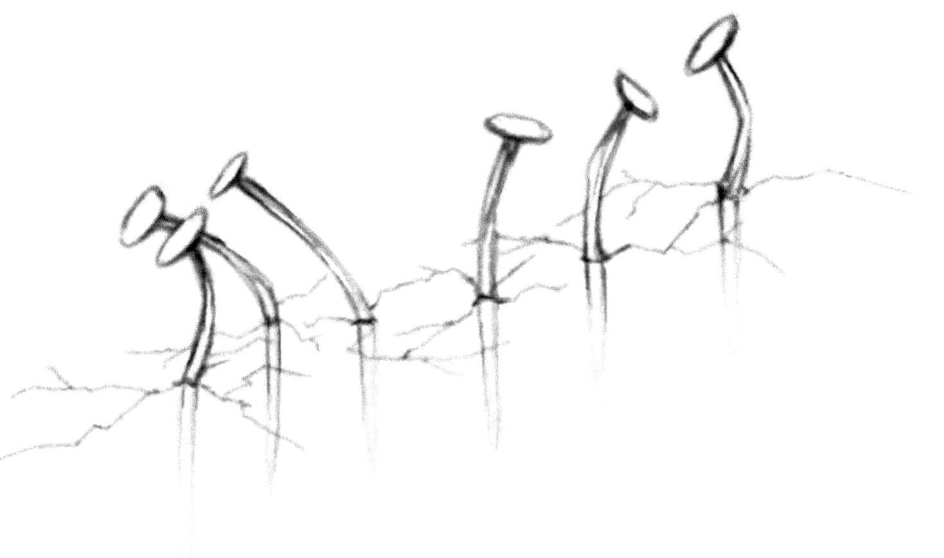

forget paint

he did not forget glass,
he remembered absence

SWEAT. *Boil.*

The sun stands over me, an adjudicating father
beating my skin to sear his mark.

Through desert sands, near metamorphosis
to glass, I drag my unfired clay body
with only the futility of my arms,
from oasis mirage to oasis mirage,

NICK CALDER

S

from oasis mirage to oasis mirage,

from oasis mirage to oasis mirage,

S WEAT. *Boil.*

from oasis mirage to *oasis mirage,*

from oasis mirage to oas

Sweat Bell

In the haze, my heat-drunken vision is tempted
by concretions of Los Angeles
dancing seductively, sated in the shade

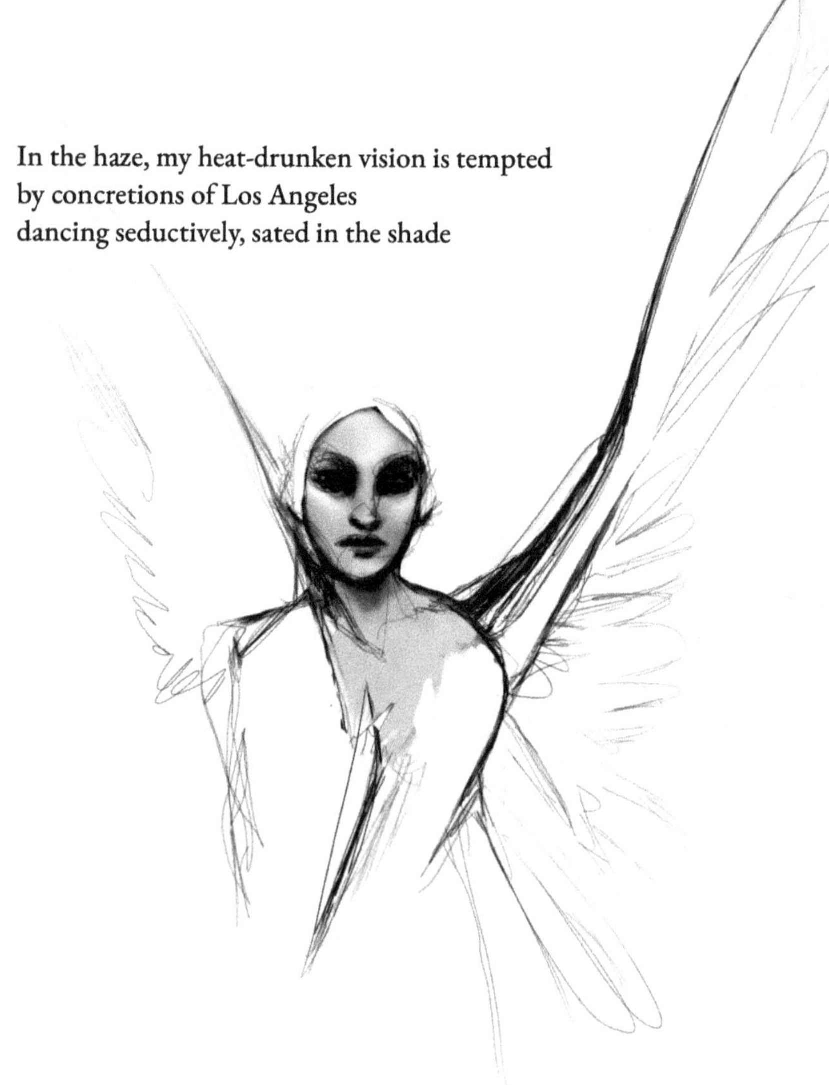

But I've tasted their tap water

I cannot stomach the chlorine

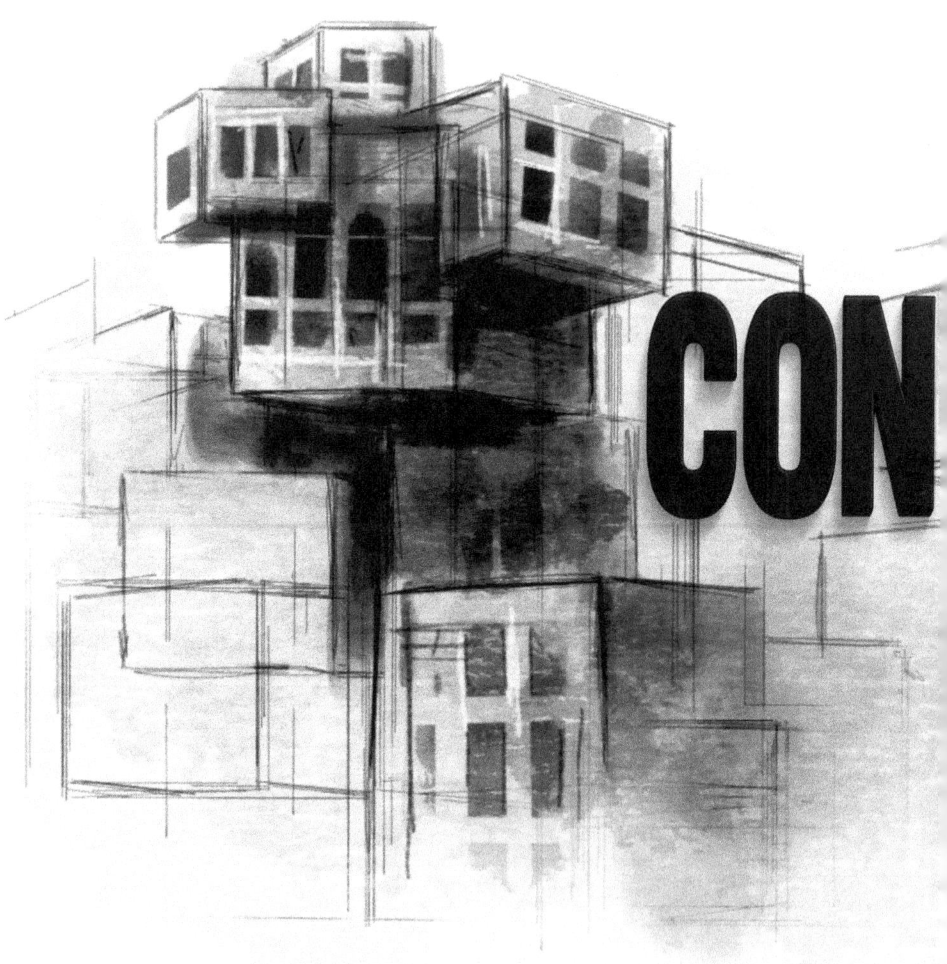
CON

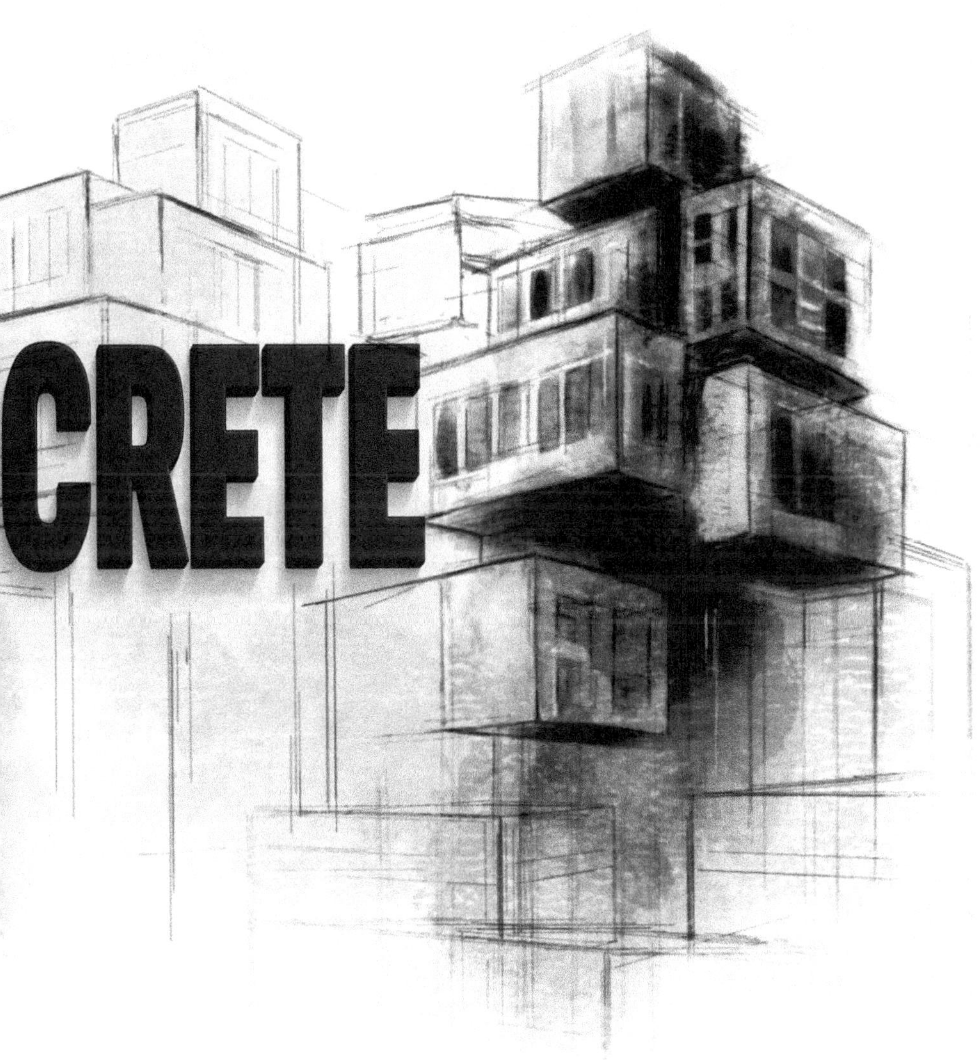

CRETE

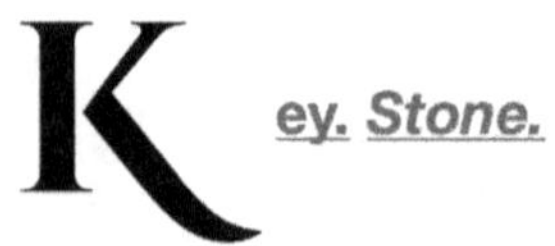

Alone, in a house
i built from bones of Home—

Anguish. mortar?
Brick balances Brick, Nick;

one window,
and too many Mirrors

one room
for me?

Two
for the Mold

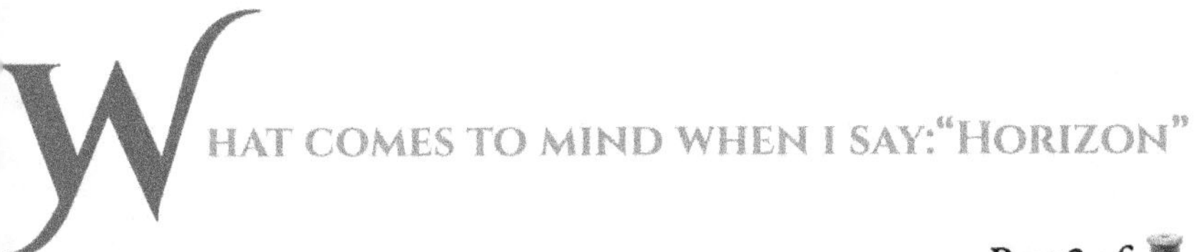 WHAT COMES TO MIND WHEN I SAY: "HORIZON"

Part 2 of 🧵

memories of sand
clenched tighter

fists only quicken
slippage

toddler-teeth only grind
loose

the gears of grandfather clocks

NICK CALDER

CHRISTMAS IN OCTOBER

with every step
another crunches

cracks and grays

brown decays. what remains
of what was. greens

CHRISTMAS MORN FEET

and standing tall
now cuddle concrete
like toddler feet
seek secondhand warmth. socks

for growing out of.
bending toddler toes
growing into
hand-me-down holes. feet

cradled in concrete

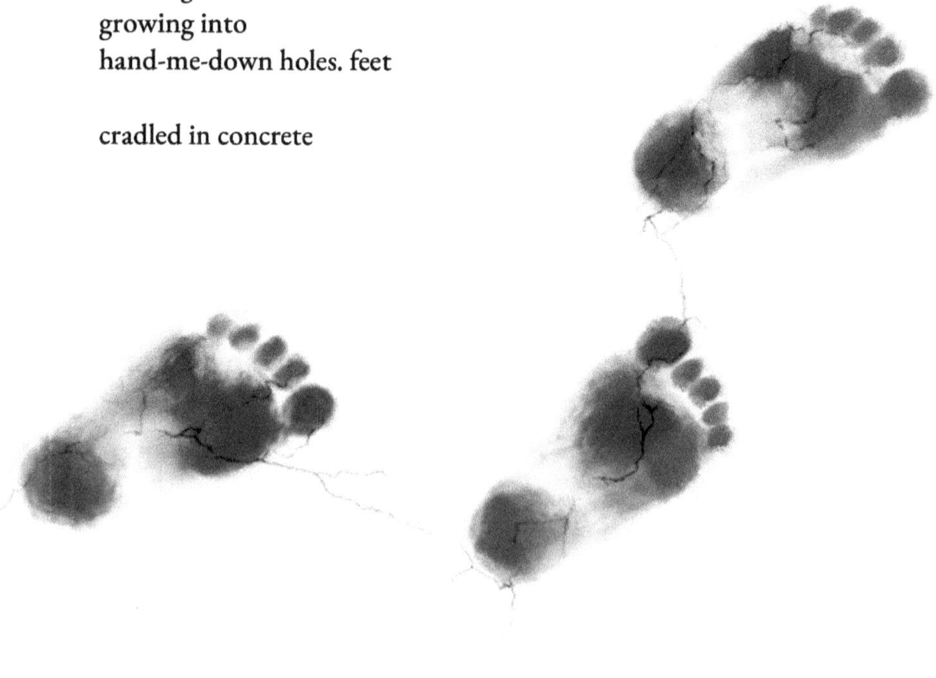

under crumbling steps
another crunches

CHRISTMAS IN OCTOBER

what's left
of what leaves

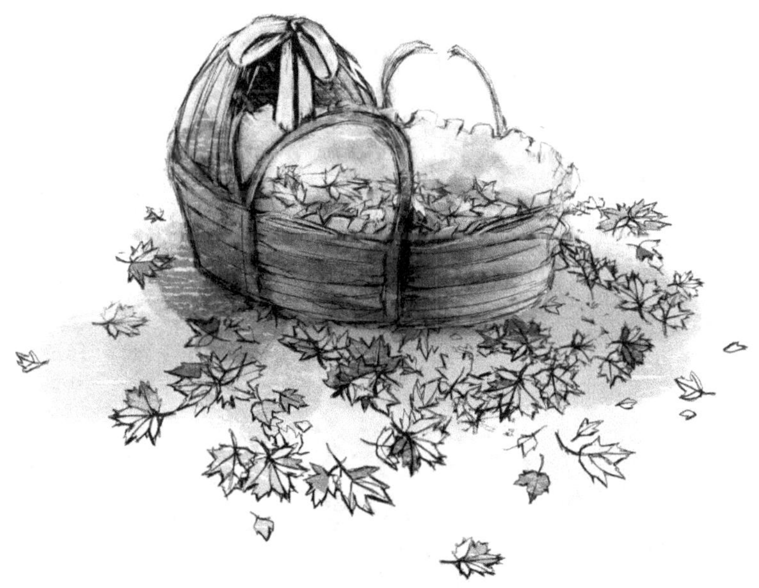

NICK CALDER

OVERGROWN

Every day was the first of Spring
Rainbows demanded no rain, only sun
Candied flowers skirted the truest paths
all of which frolicked towards immortally green trees

Roughly the length of a young boy
's attention span shallow
into the sprightly forest
thrived a communist democracy

simultaneously concealed and defined
by intangible barriers
which were eternally contested
(a fortiori when they weren't forgotten)

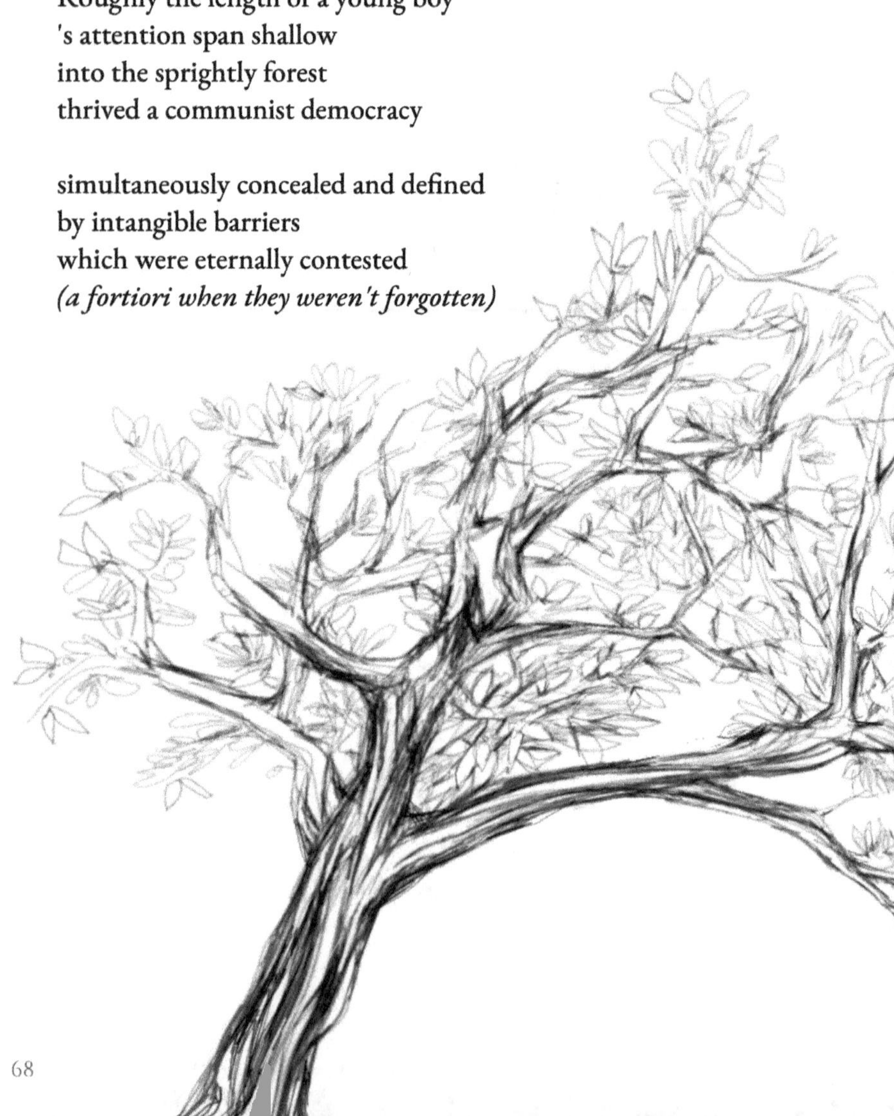

Under the forest's cover, a solitary family bound
by amorphous rules and win conditions
and conflicts of interest
made everything that never happened
      happen.

Andrew lazed like a Sloth
Austin slithered like a Snake
Nick waddled like a Penguin
Patrick ruled as 'Lord of the Undergrowth'

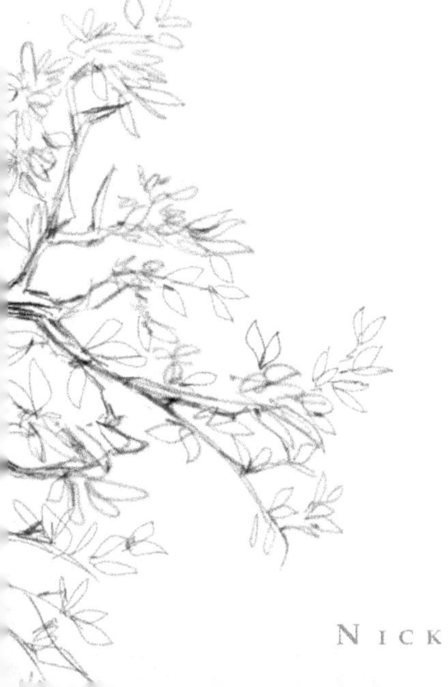

The Undergrowth that fiended for defense from the
friendly Ogre: Colin
had a penchant for basketball
and nestled under the Penguin's wing

Lounging in circles, the Sloth, Ogre, and Snake
would smoke away the Undergrowth's weed problem
while the Penguin would pretend
he was a musician

OVERBORN

He was a poet. Or philosopher.
Rarely was he ever a normal person.
Nick the Boy only existed outside the barrier
where the Boogieman named Monotony brooded

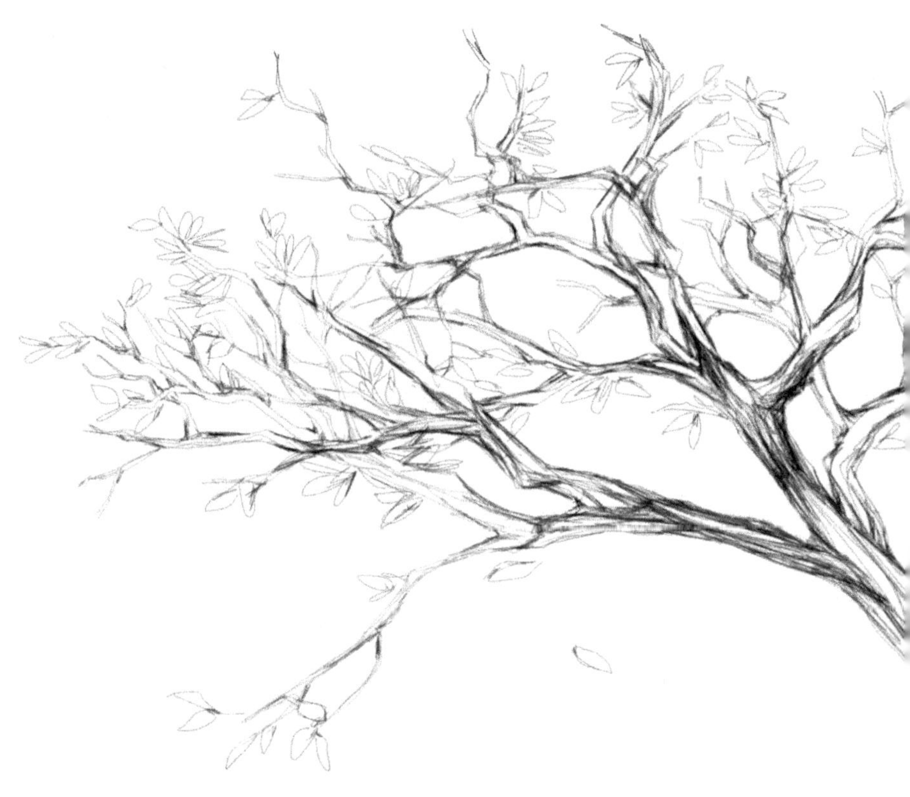

The Sloth, the Snake, the Penguin, the Lord, and the Ogre
never anticipated meeting him

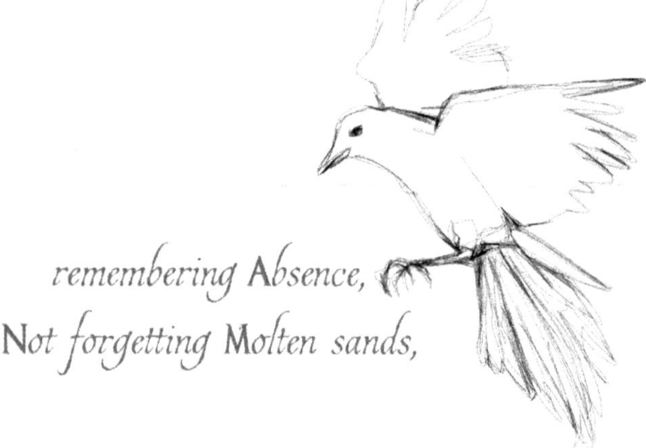

remembering Absence,
Not forgetting Molten sands,

Forget Pain

WEDNESDAY'S PROMPT IS: "HORIZON"

Part 3 of 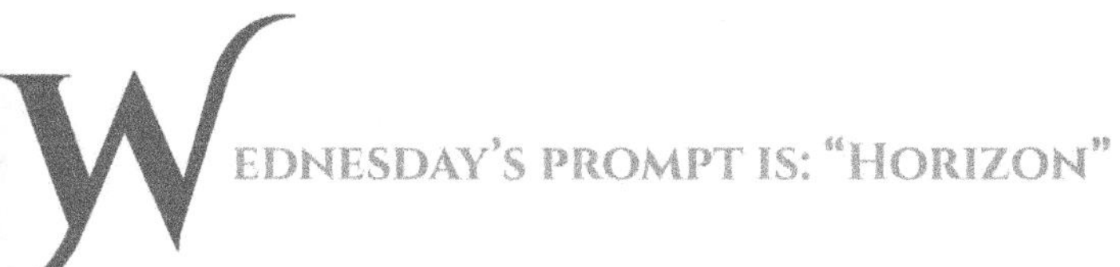

heartbeats echo in hollows between

NICK CALDER

UNDERGROWTH

Rusted metal requiems
echo off rotted wood
as Nick rakes the dead leaves
aimless over concrete floors

echoes persist eternally
buoyed by the emptiness
that shelters no vehicles
(Nick has gotten where he's going)

Once upon Spring, Undergrowth
was flourishing in conflict
with Ogres, and weeds
songs and Sloths and Snakes.

then.

Necessity screamed "Extinction!"
Nick gnawed the Overgrowth's limbs
nailed together its corpse
and manufactured a garage

he never managed to fill.

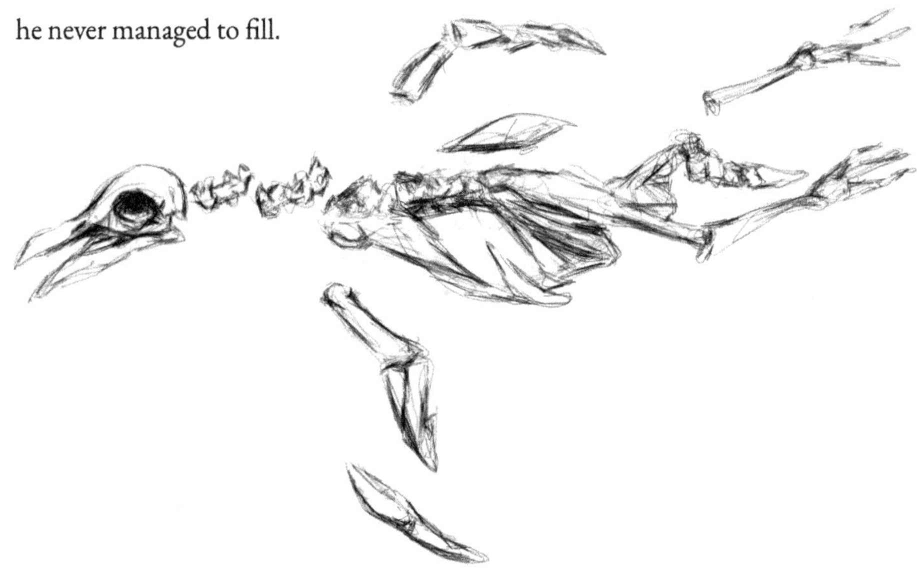

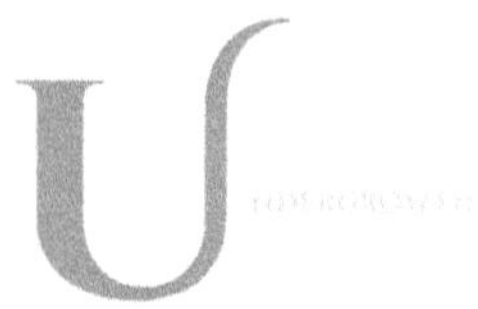

Save for a Fawn-head wall-mount
with dried blood caked below its eyes.
Strangling its neck, a lonesome adornment

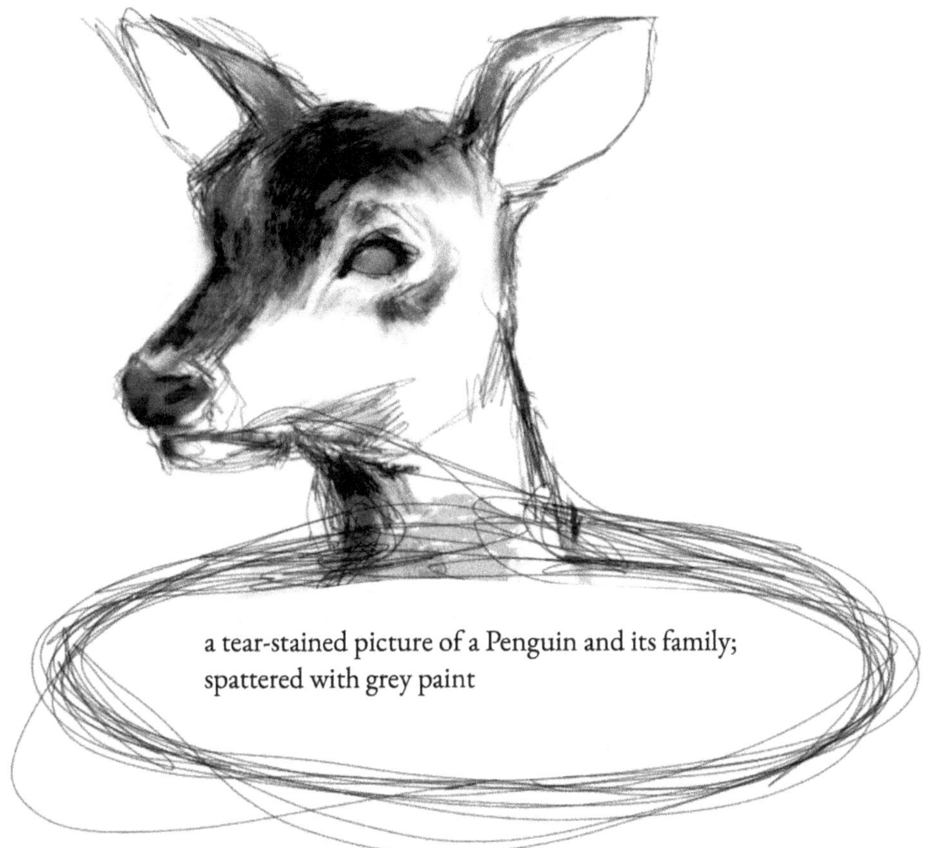

a tear-stained picture of a Penguin and its family;
spattered with grey paint

Perennial Patterns

WAKE UP!

palpitations
quaking
fabrications
of self
    sober   ?
    self-aware   ?
    successful   strong   ?   ?

bles

Crum   .

DEMOLISHED

"Go to hell!" I holler
at the demolition crew
strolling away with the shreds
of the playground I took for granted

All they left are broken pieces
of wood you're led to believe will save
you if you lose your
grip and fall
Lies.
They're splinters
from a boy's first bat
that was broken over his back
by a mother who resented him for being alive

D UNDEFINED

I refuse the monkey bars are bygone,

demolished, I reach

I grab for   them   "One   last time,"

I plead to the absence of deaf ears.

A school-teacher places a sign,

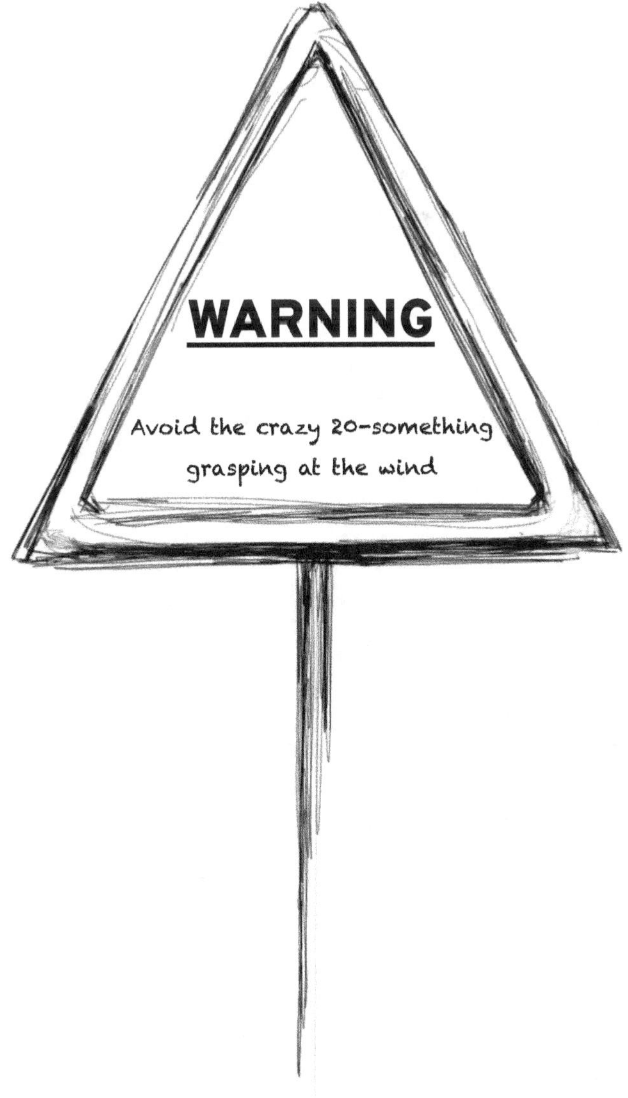
WARNING

Avoid the crazy 20-something
grasping at the wind

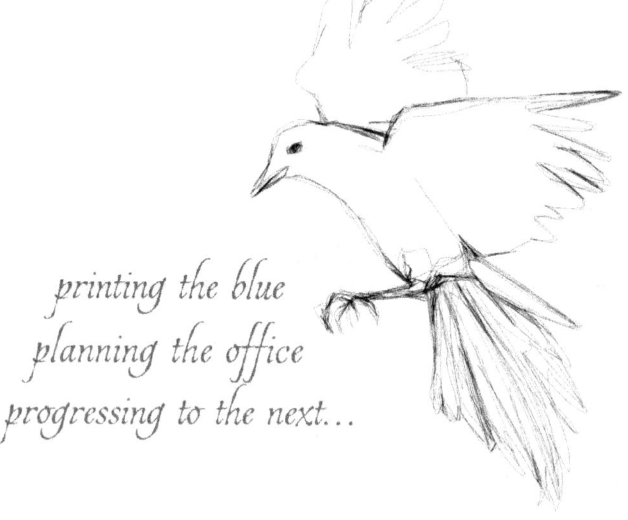

printing the blue
planning the office
progressing to the next...

GROUNDED

Clenching nostalgia
in the deep etchings of my palm;
an old friend from elementary years,
a forlorn wood chip

NICK CALDER

GROUNDED

With the tender air of a forgiven grudge
I breathe, "Why didn't you soften the fall?"
He knows 'the fall;' an old friend
has no need for specifics in questions

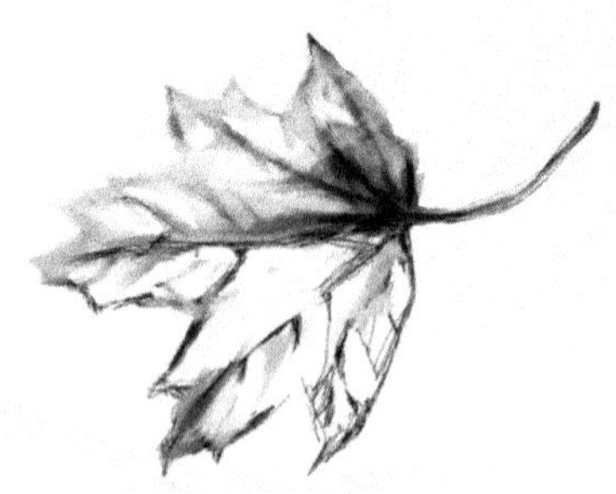

nor words in answers. As a child, I clung
to monkey bars, whose colors never stopped changing.
I swung from vibrant to vivid to vivacious,
grasping each rung like it was life

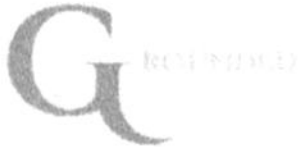

but I had never lived before.
I had never lost my grip. I had never fallen.

Now I know
how much tighter I should have clung.

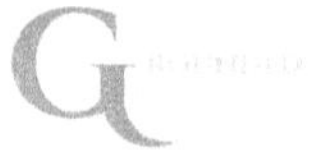

I embrace old friends that much tighter.

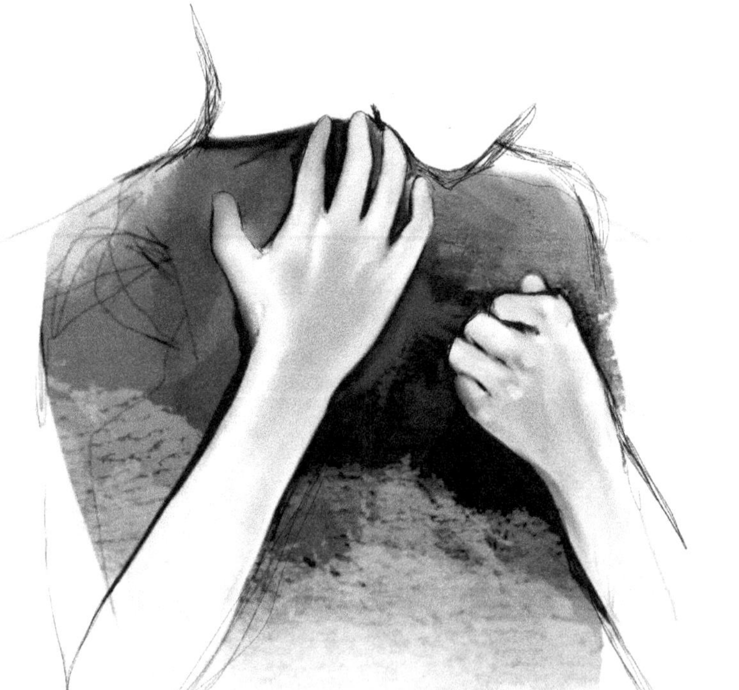

Part 4 of

the edge of everything else

and fears of losing grip

NICK CALDER

Loosey.   *I'm*   *"Home"*

                        my knuckles whiten,   bending
            backwards.   plastic connections   stressing
past   your   'intelligent design.'   Falling,   knocking
            knees thunder,   "instability;"   crashingrounding.
                                                                where corpses of Lightning
                                                                                        lie

            with skeletons of 'Safe;' still smoldering
            where scorchings of wood chips   smoke   like
            filters of cigarettes that fail   to soft
-en my regrets. one broken   loosey.   hung limp
                                                                where cancer from Lovers'
                                                                                        lies

still linger on my lip.   a Last Kiss.   frag
            ments of blistered remembrance;   play
            -ground wood chips, crushing in   praying
            palms.   I pray they etch into my prints
                                                                        as if   I
                                                pray.

                                        an ember of nostalgia
                  brands "Home" into my   lungs
                                    as if   I
                                                        believe

   'heaven' is a mantle; holding a sacred space
   for one lonely   b r oke n vas e,   annealing,   devoted
   to the fireplace. every cra ck   and   every   break   belong
   ing. meaning. brimming. loving. filled. by it

                              self
                                                   as if   I
                 believe.

                                 "Home" is where
                                            the   ashes
                                                          live
                                     as if
                                                  I.
            "Hope"?   any empty   vessel
                                     can be   an urn.

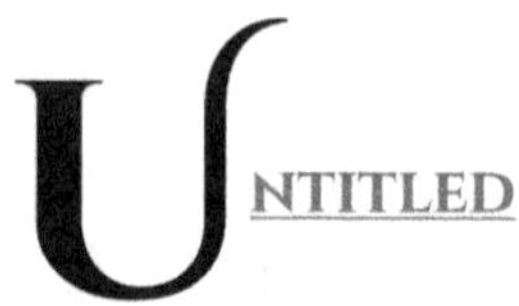

Untitled

your legacy is not
your catalog or
discography or
estate or
family name or
mausoleum of

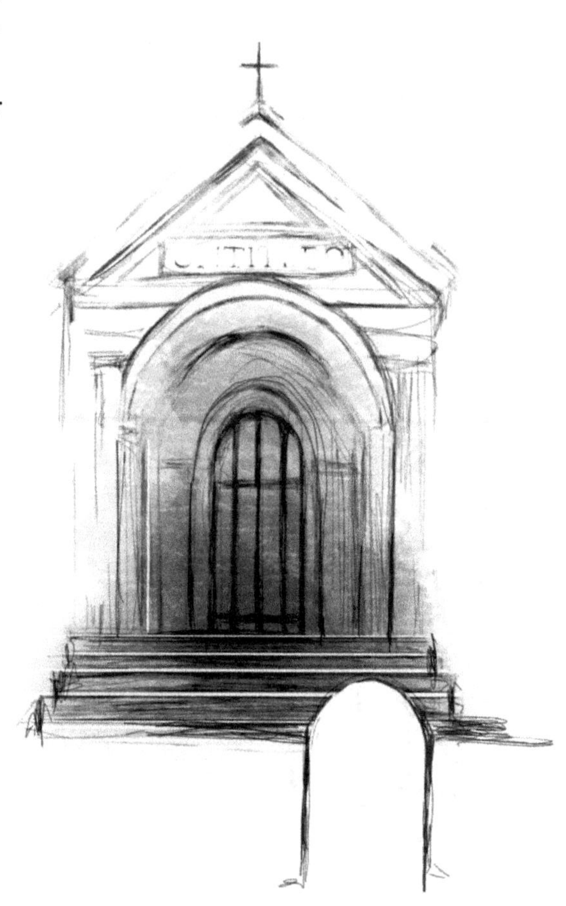

what is left of
what has left

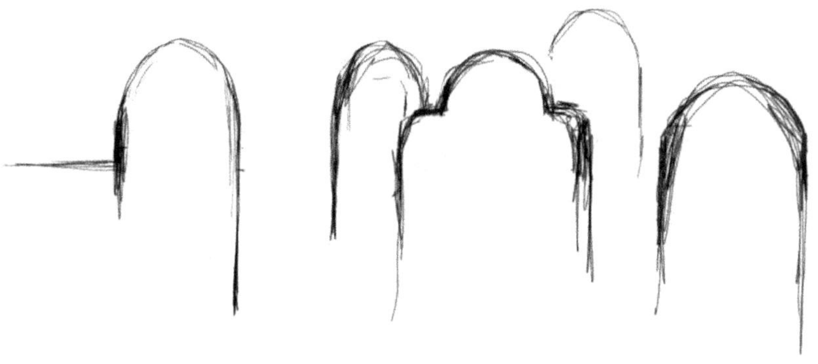

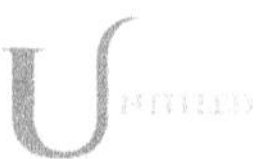

it is the fleeting flickers
of the flame they forge
when the ashes above
the fireplace rekindle
your face

GLASS
AND
GRAVEL

Copyrights

TAKING INVENTORY

Varicose asphalt veins
Asthmatic Concrete lungs
Mourning metal birds

'HORIZON

a jagged line devours the sea
stitching a seam in threads of fire.

I bystand barefoot on blistered earth
tasting the wind; *rust from distant storms*

memories of sand
clenched tighter

fists only quicken slippage

toddler teeth only grind
loose

the gears
of grandfather clocks

heartbeats   *heartbeats*

the edge of everything else

                              and fears of losing

N I C K   C A L D E R

GLASS AND GRAVEL

grip

( )S RISE | ( )S SET

sun
crackles at
her third croissant
this morning. coffee. cream

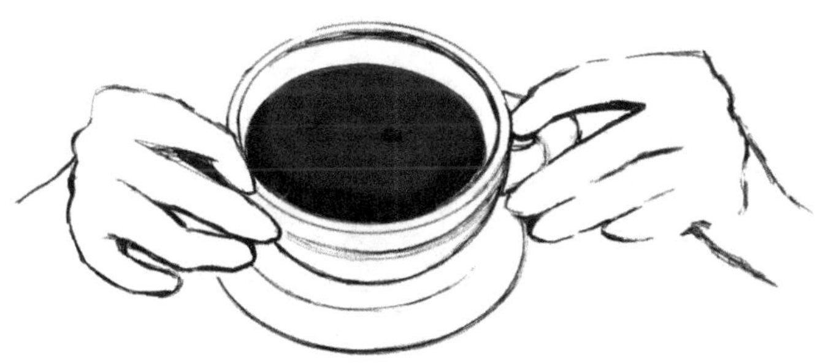

NICK CALDER

ated remains. candles creaking
Fatale~ under toe
steps. lurk.
act

ions;
fatty callouses.
flakes; four croissants
this mourning. coffee. crisco.

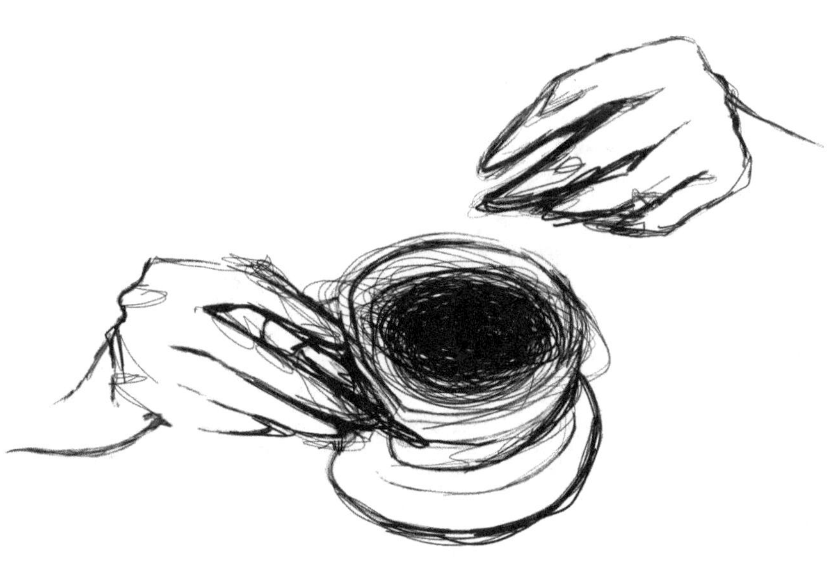

GLASS
—AND—
GRAVEL

Nick Calder

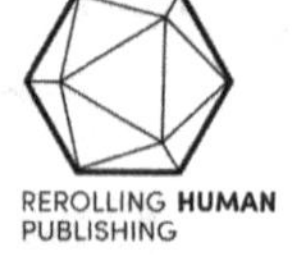

REROLLING **HUMAN**
PUBLISHING

DEDICATION

Thank you to all you before me who put your truth into the world, despite the risks, in the hope that it would help someone else. This book is only possible because of your sacrifices, and is one of my attempts at paying it forward.

Thank you to all you who supported me despite my flaws, and when I had nothing to offer you.

Thank you to all you who helped in the creation of this book, directly or indirectly.

Thank you to all you who believed me, or believed in me, when no one else did.

I couldn't have done this without you.
I know who you are.

Thank you to all you who chose to smear my name, despite your own guilt, in the hopes that you would benefit at my expense. The pain in this book is because of your lies. The successes in it are because I refused to pay it forward.

Thank you to all you who didn't believe me, or believe in me, because no one else did.

Thank you to all you who blamed me despite my innocence, when all I did was offer you everything I had.

Thank you to all you who earned my trust, only to use it against me.

You knew I'd do this without you.
You did all you could to destroy me.
You succeeded. This is the result

I KNOW WHO I AM.

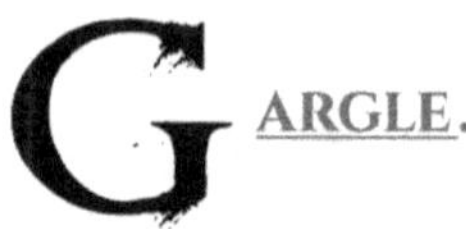

GARGLE.

I saw it first in a slit throat～
a shimmer, a fragile gasp,
light trapped in split skin,

a late apology
still bleeding.

Pain doesn't glisten.
It does itch. It does gnaw
bare its teeth
dare you to flinch

Yet in still-life,
a bead of light quivered—
clung to the bleeding neck,
a captive whisper
escaped a cage of screams

G

priests and poets
crown it

'HOPE'

but survival bears the burden

ragged, feral
picking, eating
its scabs
too stubborn to die

G

too forgiving
to stay alive

NICK CALDER

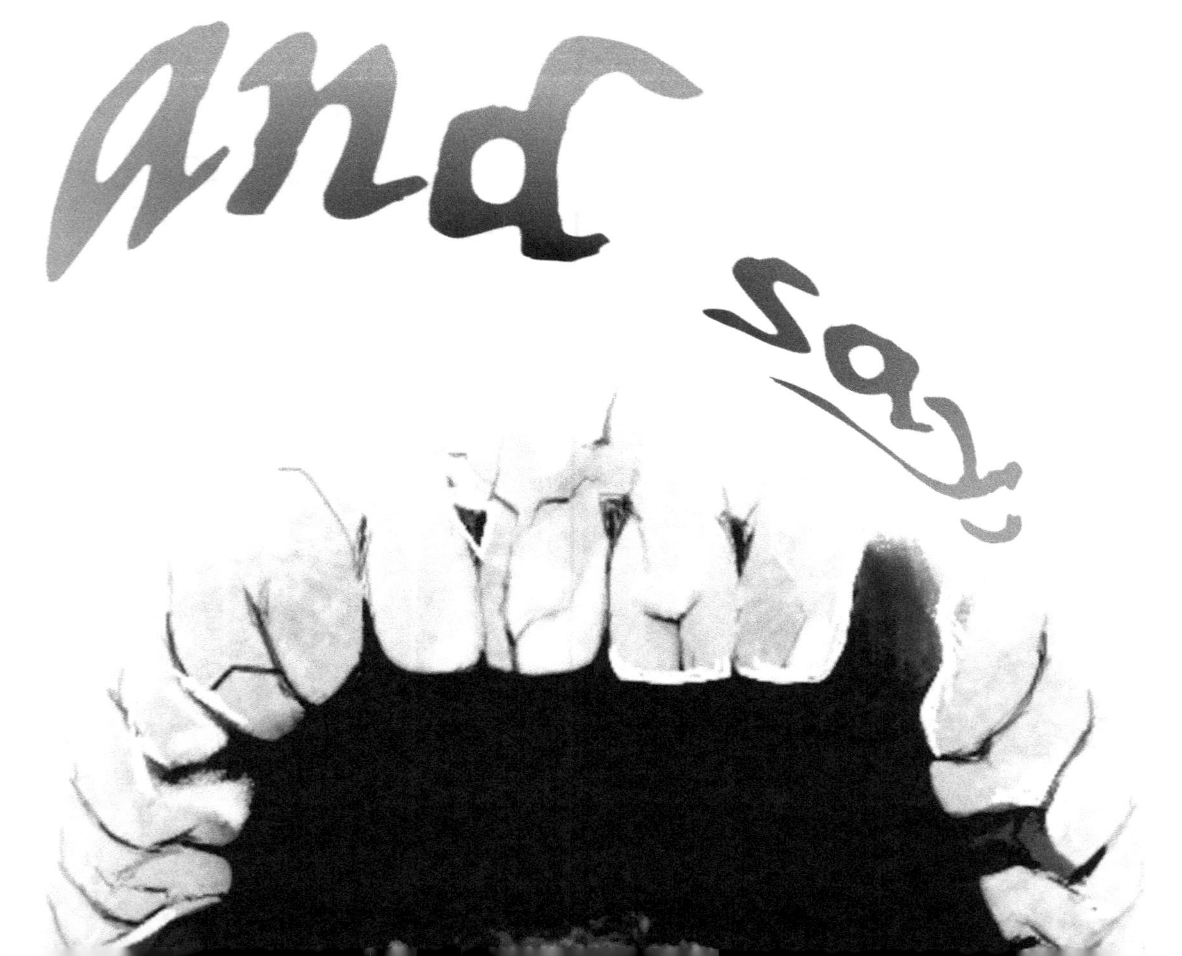

and say

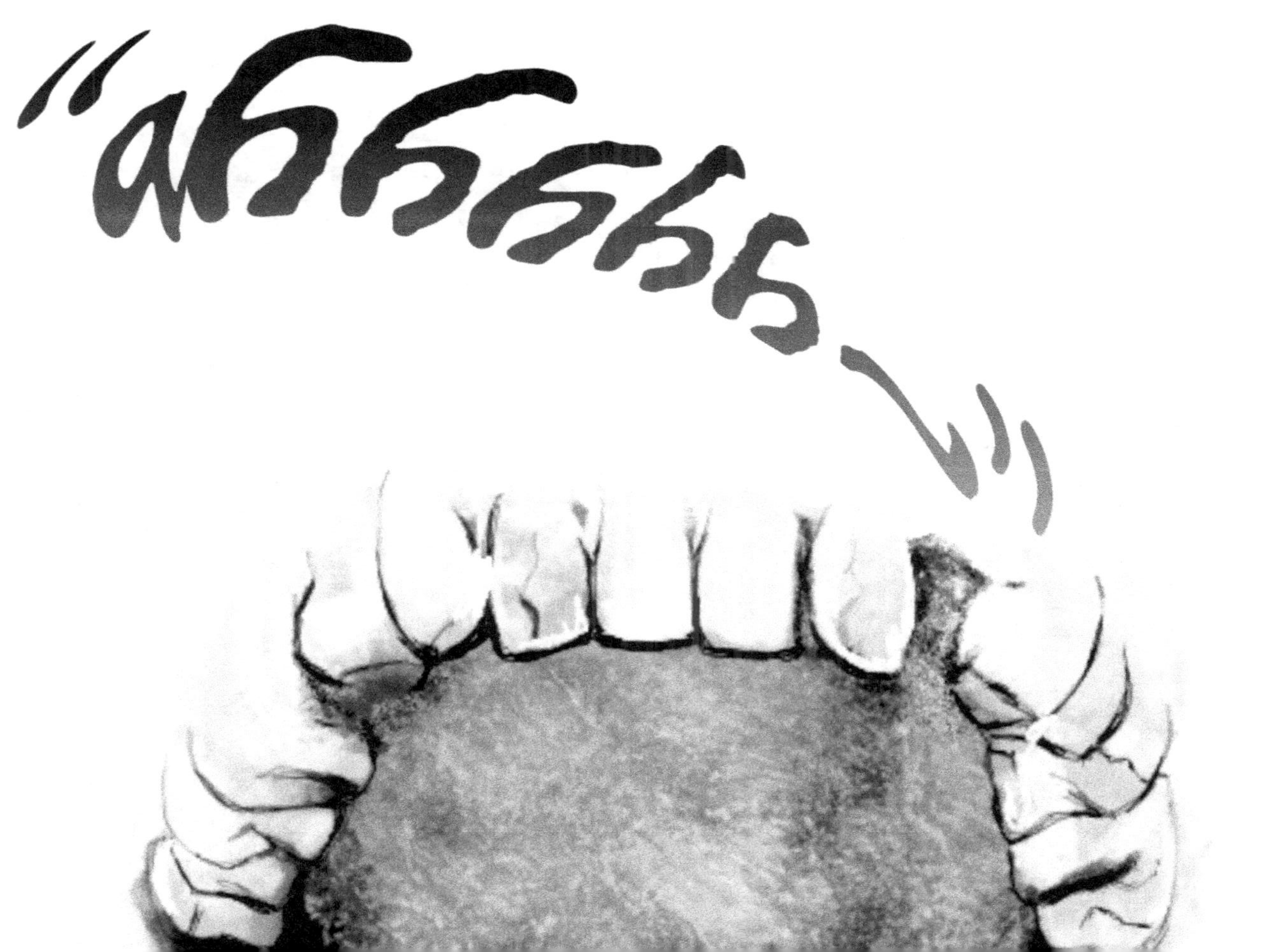
"abbbbbb

<u>**If you enjoyed this book, please help me reach others.**</u>

Who are the most famous poets you can think of?

Almost anyone you name was either broke and unknown while they were alive or worked another full-time job. Recently, some poets have found success via social media. But at the end of the day, books like *Glass and Gravel* live or die by word of mouth. Unlike typical emerging writers, I don't have a corporation behind me driving sales and exposure. But I do have you.

If this book meant something to you or if you would like to support me—consider leaving a review where you bought it, or wherever you are comfortable.

Your words don't have to be polished. They just have to be yours.

—Nick
(Amazon, Goodreads, or wherever else people still talk about books)

You can also support me or learn more about me by following me on social media (links below).
Use the hashtag #glassandgravel to connect with me and others.

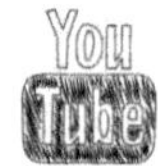

@nickcalder_   @rerollinghuman   @nickcalder

I had always written for me and never had plans to publish. I am truly doing all this because I believe there are people out there who could benefit from reading my work and because it enables me to help other writers and artists. Any and all support is greatly appreciated. And now that the sentimental piece has been written, I am happy to announce...

On the next page, you will find a hard pivot to self-deprecating humor, satire, and best of all:

bribery!

FACT:
99% of People DON'T Like Money

I'm an author - authors *hate* money. That's why we get English degrees.
Poets? *SUPER*-hate money. We refuse to eat if we have to pay.
Take that statement at face value. Don't think further into it. *Let us have this.*

But, you? Are you *different?* Dare I say... *younique?*

Are **YOU** part of the **VERY $PECIAL 1%** who <u>does</u> like **MONEY?**

You are?!

Wow!!!!!!!!!

Instructions for Reader: Blow air horn.

(Air horn not included)

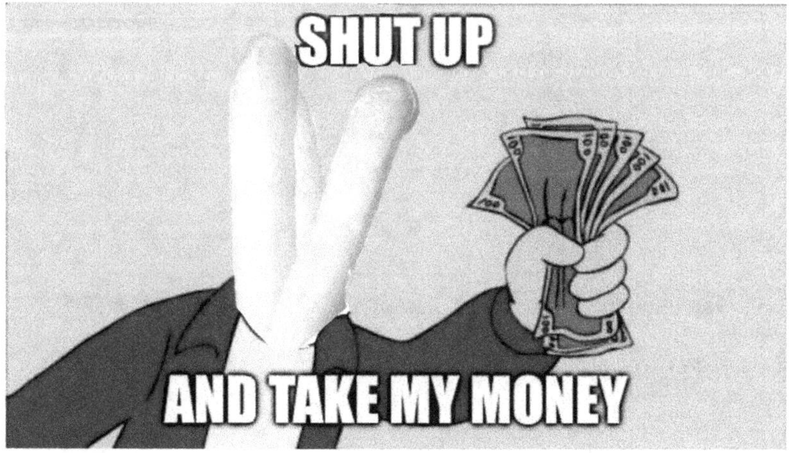

$eriously.

TURN to the NEXT PAGE to learn THREE EA$Y WAY$ to earn CA$H!

CLAIM YOUR MONEY HERE!

(It's not clickbait if it's in a book)

What you'll need:
Paypal Account | A first and last name | Ability to read | Fingers
(preferably yours)

VALUE PACKAGE	PREFERRED PACKAGE	PREMIUM DELUXE
($) REFER A FRIEND	**($$)** BOOKSTORE DISPLAY	**($$$)** BOOKSTORE STOCK
Get a friend to buy G&G	Convince a bookstore to put this book on display	Convince a bookstore to stock this book
Keep both receipts.	Make sure they know your first+last name and Paypal handle or E-mail	(10+ wholesale copies) Your first+last and Paypal
Submit form with:	Bookstore completes form with:	Bookstore completes form with:
- Yours and their receipt - Both names + e-mails - Referrer's Paypal handle or E-mail	- Photo of display - Store name + location - YOUR first + last name - YOUR Paypal account handle or e-mail	- Invoice/Receipt - Store name + location - YOUR first + last name - YOUR Paypal account handle or email
Payout? **$5!***	**Payout?!** **$10!!**	**Payout?!?!** **$20!!!**

Ready to take YOUR first step towards becoming a BILLIONAIRE?!

Scan here to submit the form!

Or follow this link: https://tally.so/r/mYyRMN

BOOKSTORES AND/OR PEOPLE WHO DIDN'T LAUGH NOT ELIGIBLE FOR REFERRAL EARNINGS.
Limit: one payout per referred person or bookstore. We verify and track each one manually.

* Paperback only. E-book referrals worth $3

Whose money am I giving you? What do you take me for, some kind of former car salesman?!

Well, I guess you *technically* gave **me** money for the book. But also to Amazon or some other tech giant disguised as a bookstore. They get most of it. Because "Infrastructure." Or, maybe it's for Jeff Bezos's razors? I hear he shaves his head 6 times a day ever since Andrew Huberman said hair might be the only thing in the way of humans achieving telekinesis.

Am I implying **Bezos is Magneto**? No. Of course not.

Has anyone thrown paper clips at him (to see if they stick) and **lived** to tell the tale?
A L S O no. Just sayin'.

For those of you re-reading this book from jail, you may be wondering;
"Why didn't he tell me it was illegal?"
I don't know. Don't blame *me* for **your** hilarious idea.
I hope this answer was worth smuggling into prison.

Anyway... referrals... am I giving you back *your* money? Are you taking *my* money? Are we *both* losing money... unless we own Amazon stocks? Does Amazon win no matter what?

To answer one or more of those questions:
Yes.

What's that? Did you just say, *"This sounds like a great idea for a book!"* in your head?
You did?! No way! I was thinking the *same* **exact** thing when I wrote this!
100 points to Readers Everywhere for "Reading" (*wink wink*) my mind
I'll call the book: *"Whose Money Is It Anyway?"*
Audiobook voiced by: Drew Carey

Don't want to wait for that? Fine. Your loss. Check out my other book here:

https://amzn.to/45amtT7   or

By now, you may have questions like "Is this guy serious?" or "How can I start a kickstarter to get his collaborators a good therapist?" and "Will I ever get answers to these questions I've been forced to ask?"

Have your cake and eat it too, *and more!* Sign up for my ~~dad jokes~~ newsletter here:

nickcalder.beehiv.com   or

Founder of Rerolling Human | Author of 'Glass and Gravel' | Author of 'MOMmy: The First Perennial Issue'

Thank you to the beta readers whose feedback and support is invaluable and consented to being mentioned in the book:

CASEY LEMING

DANNY SRP

MICHAEL HINTON

And a huge thank you to those who played a major role in the creation of this book. If you enjoyed their contributions, please consider supporting them by hiring them for your own projects. Each of them are wonderful to collaborate with, and went above and beyond what would normally be expected of them for a project like this.

Find how to contact them, and a statement from each of them, on this page or the next:

<u>CLARA VECCHI</u>
ILLUSTRATOR

"These images weren't made with the intention of clarifying the poems, or to soften them.
They were made inside the confusion, the rupture, the silence between words.
Some of them look unfinished. Some of them are. Some others are distorted, torn apart, scribbled on;
echoes of the chaos that is threaded through the pages.
They don't speak about beauty, only the ghost of it.
The fragile remains of something once whole, eroding beneath the weight of exposure."

https://claravecchi.my.canva.site/

Nick Calder is the founder of Rerolling Human Publishing House, co-leader of JPS (a local poetry club), and author of Glass and Gravel. His form-breaking poetry has gained renown for being visceral, disruptive, and unflinching. Outside of his literary pursuits, you can find him listening to music at a local coffee shop. Or, if their menu has more than one size of cappuccino, leaving a local coffee shop. Visit him at nickcalderauthor.com to learn more, and join the newsletter for behind-the-scenes content.

nickcalderauthor.com

rerollinghuman.com

Author Newsletter Signup

Other Work by The Author

1. Beulah Amsterdam (1972). "Mirror self-image reactions before age two". Developmental Psychobiology. 5 (4): 297–305. doi:10.1002/dev.420050403. PMID 4679817.

2. Prior, H.; Schwarz, A.; Güntürkün, O. (2008). "Mirror-induced behavior in the magpie (Pica pica): Evidence of self-recognition". PLOS Biology. 6 (8): e202. doi:10.1371/journal.pbio.0060202. PMC 2517622. PMID 18715117.

* :‖

† ‖:

www.ingramcontent.com/pod-product-compliance
Lightning Source LLC
Chambersburg PA
CBHW071443130726
47997CB00006B/2216